The Joy

# of Junk

Cheryl Fall

Please call or write for our free catalog of publications. To place an order or obtain a free catalog, please call 800-258-0929. Please use our regular business telephone, 715-445-2214, for editorial comment or further information.

kp krause publications
An F&W Publications Company

700 East State Street • Iola, WI 54990-0001
715-445-2214 • 888-457-2873
www.krause.com

Library of Congress Catalog Number 2003101331
ISBN 0-87349-615-9

This book is dedicated to my parents, who taught me how to fix just about everything ....

Special thanks to my husband, Tony, and daughters Becca and Ashley, for letting me take over the garage so I didn't scatter my creative messes throughout the house.

To Mary Nevius for the gorgeous photography, her friendship, and Web site building expertise.

And to Christine Townsend, an outstanding editor and fellow junk lover, Jamie Griffin for the wonderful design layout, and Julie Stephanie, acquisitions editor and sounding board. You're all wonderful!

—Cheryl Fall

The Joy of Junk

by Cheryl Fall

Chapter 5: Recycled Romance 69

Chapter 6: Creative Flourishes 89

Chapter 7: Secondhand Savvy 107

Chapter 8: Cleaning & Restoration 122

Appendix: Resources 126
Index 127

C H A P T E R 1

The Thrill of the Hunt: Finding the Good Stuff

I adore junk. Not for what it is, but for what it can become. I also enjoy the hunt for it. Many of my junking forays yield absolutely nothing, but when I come across a wonderful find, it's exhilarating! I guess you could say I'm a "junk junkie."

If you have thumbed through the myriad of home décor magazines lately, or visited chic decorating stores, you'll see a penchant for a casual, shabby style. It's an eclectic mix of old and new, refurbished and well-worn, timeless and timely. It's a comfy, cozy look that everyone has been adapting in one form or another—but most have paid retail prices for the worn-out look.

In this book, I'm going to show you how to turn ordinary junk into chic treasures for your home. But first, you'll need to know where to *find* great junk!

Where to Find the Good Stuff

Locating great junk isn't difficult, and it's a lot of fun. All you need to get started is a tank full of gas, cash in small denominations, and a sense of adventure. Leave your credit cards and check book at home—most sales won't accept them.

You can head out alone, as I do, or bring along a friend or two. You can even bring your hubby if he's the patient, adventurous type—my hubby prefers to remain in the car, but he'll come out occasionally if he sees tools.

Dress casually, appropriately for the weather, and wear comfy shoes. Keep a few cardboard boxes or grocery sacks in your car; some sales don't provide bags so yours will come in handy if you find lots of stuff. You can also use them to cushion breakables for the journey home in the back of your car. Once you're a seasoned "junk junkie," you'll also find you need to bring along rope, old moving blankets, and masking tape.

Flea markets and swap meets are the "mother lode" for die-hard junk collectors. I know of people who visit flea markets all across the nation. At these sales, you'll find row after row of junk at great prices. Don't be in a hurry when you visit these sales. Take your time so you don't miss anything! Plan to spend an entire day there. Pack a lunch of you want to, and keep it in a cooler in your trunk.

Don't bring a purse. Instead, carry a small coin purse or wallet in your front pocket (to deter pickpockets, who tend to frequent these events), and bring along a backpack so you can carry your smaller finds but keep your hands free for the larger ones. Stuff a few plastic grocery bags in your pack—you never know when you'll need them, and they weigh almost nothing.

Visit each and every stall, and peer into every box and crate. There's great stuff hiding in there! Be prepared to bargain. It's not only the way to get stuff at the best price, it's also expected of you. Some vendors will take as much as forty percent off the asking price if you play your cards right— but be realistic with your offers; don't insult the sellers.

Secondhand Stores and Estate Sales

Secondhand stores, also known as thrift stores, are where I find many of my favorite bargains. You'll find great junk for a song: $5 for an antique chair, 99¢ for a set of wine glasses, or $1.99 for a silver plated tray in perfect condition. Secondhand stores can also be a fabulous place to find valuable collectibles such as Depression glass and vintage textiles.

A word to the wise: Professional "antiquers" also know the value of secondhand and thrift stores. These folks are the ones waiting at the door before the doors even open! In fact, this is where they usually find the "antiques and collectibles" for their stores or online auctions.

The pros choose the store to visit based on when the trucks of merchandise arrive. You can do the same thing—all you need to do is ask the store manager which days are best for new merchandise. Typically, the merchandise on a truck is put on the floor the day following its arrival.

Your best bet is to get there before the doors open in the morning. When they do, *run* (don't walk) to the section of the store you are most interested in, or you'll miss out on the best stuff. Professionals swoop through the store like vultures, picking up anything of value before anyone else can get it. This isn't the time to be polite—great junk goes fast!

Estate sales are also great sources of junk … where else can you find an entire household of junk in *one* location? You'll find a lifetime of accumulation under one roof—everything from kitchen, dining, and bedroom items to tools and sporting equipment. However, prices can be a little high. I'm often amazed at the prices of items that will be heading for the secondhand store at the end of the sale. A dresser could have a price tag of $150 at the estate sale, but once the item enters the thrift store it's marked down to $30.

Some estate sales mark everything down on the last day of the sale—the best day to go. You could also try making offers to the sellers on the last day, because they know that anything is better than nothing—which is exactly what the sellers will get if they send the remaining loot to the local thrift store.

Professional Junk Sales

Barn and farm sales are fun. Auction houses run many of them. I like to head out early and enjoy the drive with a thermos full of hot coffee and a bag of donuts (I have to have the donuts). These sales are fabulous if you're looking for vintage items such as old furniture, interesting tools, or farm equipment. Tractor wheels make great yard sculptures, as do old wagons, tillers, and cider presses.

Barns sales can get crowded. There's something nostalgic about a sale at an old farm that draws folks like a magnet. Some are there to buy, others are there just because they took a drive on a nice morning and saw the sign (I must admit, some of my most fortuitous finds were "on the fly"—just passin' through, folks).

The majority of farm and barn sales are one-time sales. However, you'll also run across the occasional farmer who likes to hold monthly or quarterly sales. These are usually worth revisiting because that farmer gathers more great junk from his neighboring farmers for his sales. You never know what you'll find—I recently found a fabulous old laundry bench, complete with two tin basins. It looks delightful filled with flowers on my front porch.

Salvage yards are great places to find unusual items: Door lintels, old moldings, and windows that can be transformed into new items such as tables and wall art. You may also find a terrific old fireplace mantle that will make the perfect headboard in your bedroom!

While salvage yards can be more expensive than other sales, you'll find a greater selection of architectural-style merchandise at them than you will anywhere else. You can find these places in the phone book under "salvage."

The Ubiquitous Yard Sale

You may be wondering, "What's the difference among yard sales, garage sales, tag sales, backyard sales, patio sales, and moving sales?" The answer is: "Absolutely nothing." They're all the same thing—just given a different name.

Some folks just seem to have an aversion to the term "yard sale" or "garage sale" and prefer to call them "tag sales." Personally, I couldn't care less what people call them—I'll still slam on the brakes when I see the "sale" sign hanging from the telephone pole (my sincere apologies to the car behind me).

There are some tag sales out there that try to operate in a manner similar to an estate sale: Only a few people are allowed in at a time, and everything is tagged. There is often no room for bargaining. I'd rather spend my nickel at you-name-the-price neighborhood yard sales!

Yard sales can be wonderful places to find junk, but can also be duds. There have been many days I head out, map and classified ads in hand, ready for the hunt. I can easily visit ten or twelve sales in one morning and go home totally exhausted and empty-handed. The reason is that some homeowners think they really have super-duper special stuff and place an exorbitant price tag on their junk. To those folks I'd like to offer this advice: Visit your local thrift stores and notice their pricing. If you don't price your stuff similarly, it'll end up in the thrift store anyway. Would you rather make a few bucks or nothing at all? Other people put items out for sale that truly belong in the garbage … empty licorice containers, water-damaged books.

It can take a lot of duds before you come across a really great yard sale—but they *are* out there. It helps to do some research ahead of time by checking the classified ads. I have found that the best sales are those that say "neighborhood" or "multi-family" in the ad. Church sales are also good sales and are worth a visit.

Creative Dumpster Diving

Sometimes truly great junk is in the trash—seriously! Even so, I really don't expect you to go diving into dumpsters; it's merely a term for finding great junk destined for the trash truck.

Have you ever been driving through your neighborhood and noticed that someone has set something out for the trash that is just too good to throw away? Perhaps it's a pretty, old side chair or folding table; it may be a metal table base that the homeowner no longer finds useful because the glass insert is broken…this is the type of junk I'm talking about.

Don't be shy, friend! Anything on the curb is fair game, in my opinion! Slam on those brakes, hop out of the car, and stuff the item in the trunk or back seat. If you're quick, no one will even see you!

If you're still a bit leery, you can always drive through neighborhoods across town—but you'll need to find out which day of the week is garbage day.

And don't be fooled into thinking the "fancy" neighborhoods have the best junk—they don't! The best curbside junk can be found in established, older neighborhoods, especially those with a larger population of senior citizens. To them, the stuff they're putting out for the trashman is just old junk that's been cluttering up their basements or garages. To us junk lovers, it's pure treasure!

Developing an Eye for the Good Stuff

As you become familiar with the junking process, you'll eventually acquire an "eye" for good "junk." You'll find yourself spending less time looking through everything and instead will tend to zero-in on the objects you're after. Some folks have a knack for it; others need time to develop the knack.

When you've developed the eye, you'll be able to pull up to the curb at a yard sale and scan the offerings without even getting out of the car. By then, you'll have learned that if it looks like a dud from the car, it probably is.

While you're eyeing junk, keep in mind its condition. Before you bring home anything, ask yourself if it can be transformed into something really neat, or repaired and used for its original purpose. Ugly, old paint or worn-out finishes can be stripped, fabric seats replaced, and hardware changed, but broken legs and missing hardware can present a problem.

While you're developing your eye, allow your imagination to grow too. Look at items from a different perspective. For example, an old iron kettle with its lid missing will make an excellent planter for a fern. Ornate picture frames can be transformed into unique tea trays or bulletin boards. Drawer knobs can become coat rack hooks or legs for a box. Don't worry—you'll get the picture—especially after you see some of the items right here in this book.

Things You Should Never Pass Up

There are certain items out there I recommend you never pass up. Either they're difficult to locate when you need them, or you just can never have too many of them!

Never pass up **glass domes** of any size. They can be used as cheese and cake covers, placed over seedling plants like old-fashioned bell jars, or turned upside down and used as punch bowls.

You can never have too many **chairs**. If you find that you do, give them to friends as gifts and find some more. Always be on the lookout for chairs with interesting legs and turnings.

Vintage textiles and **linens** are also worth bringing home. These items can be transformed into pillows, used to recover chairs, or used for their original intent. Vintage textiles have a lovely, soft texture and subdued colors, making them perfect choices for home décor.

Hardware and other "findings" are things you should also bring home with you. These include doorknobs, hooks, faceplates, hinges, buttons, silverware, laces, trims, and ribbons. You'll always have a use for these items.

Interesting **bottles** and **jars** are also great finds. They can be used to store items in your home, from bath salts to bread flour. They also make great impromptu candleholders and flower vases.

Carved wooden frames are also must-have items. You can use them for their original purpose or adapt them for use as trays, cork and bulletin boards, tabletops, and more.

Now, on to the projects.

CHAPTER 2

Flea Market Makeovers

Refreshed Library Table

When I came across this old desk at a junk sale, it was covered in many thick, drippy layers of old paint. After giving it some "quality time" with heavy gloves, a scraper, and furniture stripping solution, things were looking great—until I stripped the drawer fronts.

After admiring the lovely grain of the wood in the legs and top, I was shocked to discover the drawers were not original to the piece and were of a lesser-quality wood. Instead of staining the piece as I had originally planned, I decided to repaint it—*properly,* and with tender, loving care.

To finish it off, I gave this piece a bit of antiquing for a lovely patina. This desk now serves as a side table in my dining room.

Materials:

- Old desk with fine, spindly legs
- Soap and water
- Replacement drawer pulls (if the originals are not going to be reused)
- Decorative wood accents for the drawers
- Jasco™ Furniture Refinisher or paint remover (if stripping item)
- Wood glue
- Americana® Satins acrylic paint (wide-mouth jar) in Sage Green
- DecoArt multi-purpose sealer
- DecoArt Americana acrylic paint in Sable Brown
- DecoArt Faux glazing medium
- DecoArt DuraClear exterior/interior varnish, satin finish
- Wood putty
- Fine sandpaper
- Assorted paintbrushes
- Electric drill

1 Remove the hardware. Clean and dry the surface of the desk. Strip it if necessary, but if the piece is in good shape, you may only need to sand it lightly. Fill any chips or cracks with wood putty. Allow the putty to dry, and sand it smooth. Wipe clean.

2 Glue the decorative wood accents to the centers of the drawers. Allow the glue to dry. Re-glue any loose joints at this time, too.

3 Apply one coat of sealer. Let the sealer dry, and sand lightly again. Wipe clean.

4 Using a good-quality brush, apply the first coat of paint and let it dry. Sand lightly, wipe clean, and apply a second coat.

5 Lightly sand the entire piece, taking off a bit of the paint at the edges to give it a well-used appearance. Wipe clean.

6 Tint a small amount of the glazing medium with an equal amount of the Sable Brown acrylic paint. Using a brush, apply the glaze onto the piece in sections, wiping off the excess with a soft cloth. Wipe off as much as desired. After antiquing the entire piece, allow it to dry.

7 Seal the entire piece using the clear satin varnish.

8 Drill new holes for the drawer pulls through the centers of the glued wood accent pieces. Install the drawer pulls.

Painted Metal Photo Frames

Make these nifty picture "frames" using old metal trays purchased for a dollar or two at tag sales and flea markets. You can even use old silver plate trays that are too worn out to be used on the table. If using silver plate, be sure to remove the tarnish before spraying with the primer.

If you would like to give your new photos an aged appearance, as I did in the samples, scan your photos and recolor them on your computer using whatever photography software was installed in your scanner. You can also enlarge and reduce, or crop and zoom in on your photos using your scanner software. The other option is to have them re-colored and resized on a color photocopier.

One can of each of the spray materials is enough for about eight frames.

Materials:

Old tray per photo, 8" to 10" in diameter
Soap and water
White spray primer
Off-white matte-finish spray paint
Faux stone- or sand-finish spray paint
Clear spray sealer
Picture to fit center area (flat area) of tray
Twine

Ribbon roses
Rubber cement
Scratch paper
Stick-on picture hangers
Hot glue gun and clear glue, or heavy-duty adhesive
Drop cloth

1 Clean the tray with hot water and soap, and allow it to dry thoroughly.

2 Cover your work surface with a drop cloth (outdoors, or in a well-ventilated area) and spray both sides of the tray with primer. Allow it to dry.

3 Spray both sides of the tray with the off-white matte paint. Allow the first side to dry thoroughly before turning the tray over and spraying the other side.

4 Cut a piece of scrap paper to fit the shape of the inside bottom (flat area) of the tray. Glue the paper to the tray with rubber cement to mask this area.

5 Spray the outer areas of the tray, front side only, with the textured paint. Peel off the paper mask immediately. Allow the tray to dry for at least 48 hours. Spray the tray, front and back, with clear sealer.

6 Cut the photo to fit the inside bottom (flat area that you had previously masked) of the tray. Glue the photo in place with rubber cement.

7 Hot-glue twine around the edges of the photo to conceal the edges of the paper. Glue ribbon roses where desired.

8 Using hot glue or heavy-duty adhesive, attach a hanger to the back side of the tray. Hang your new frames on the wall, or place in a plate stand and enjoy!

Decaled What Not Box

Every home needs a what not box—a place to keep whatever needs keeping. I like to keep mine in the kitchen. I use it to store all the recipes and coupons I clip from the paper and recipe cards given to me by friends and neighbors. Dig to the bottom and you'll also find twist-ties, paper clips, and a button or two.

The box is actually new. It came from the craft supply store. It's the legs and handle that are junk. I found a bag full of old porcelain knobs at an estate sale. They were absolutely charming, and the bag contained about thirty knobs in varying sizes. They're the old-fashioned-type, with a screw that goes directly through the knob—not like the new variety with screws countersunk into the backside of the knob. I often wonder where they came from. I'm guessing, due to the bright white color of the porcelain, that they were from an old apothecary chest.

Cheryl's Tip:
Another nifty idea would be to découpage the box with old recipes—similar to the Fabulous Rehab Storage Boxes shown in the next project.

Materials:

Unfinished wooden box with hinged lid, any size
Delta Ceramcoat® all-purpose sealer
Delta Ceramcoat® acrylic paint, Light Ivory
Delta Ceramcoat® interior varnish, satin finish
5 white porcelain knobs

Provo Craft® First Impressions rub-on transfer, any style measuring 5-1/4" x 22-1/2"
Fine sandpaper
Assorted paintbrushes
Trimming knife
Rags
Scissors

1 Lightly sand the box to remove any imperfections. Wipe clean. Seal it with a coat of the all-purpose sealer and let it dry.

2 Apply two coats of the white paint to the box, letting it dry between coats.

3 Seal the box with the satin varnish. Let it dry overnight. Make sure it is thoroughly dry and not tacky to the touch.

4 If you are using the herbal transfers like the box in the sample, cut with scissors the band of lettering from the bottom of each transfer and set aside. Cut out the rub-on transfers 1/4" from the edges. Following the directions on the transfer package, rub the transfers into position on the sides of the box.

5 Apply the lettering to the top of the box, near the edge, directly over each transfer you placed on the sides. Make sure you give the correct name to each herb! These are permanent decals, so you only get one chance.

6 If your decals happen to cover the seam where the lid meets the box, use the knife to carefully slice along the area where to two points meet.

7 Give the box one more coat of satin varnish and let it dry.

8 Attach the knob legs to the bottom of the box. Attach the fifth knob to the lid.

Fabulous Rehab Storage

I'm a bit of a pack rat. After cleaning out the storage closet under the stairs, I came across a cache of lidded boxes. After staring at them for a few days, I decided they'd make great storage boxes for my husband's office, once they were rehabilitated. The various sizes of the boxes would be wonderful for organizing desk materials, from paper and CD cases to pencils and paper clips.

Another quick search through my stash, and I had the perfect covering material for them—an old Canadian history book from 1947 that was beyond repair (and certainly out of date). If you don't have a suitable old book, you can use wrapping paper, plain brown paper, maps, newspapers, or magazines.

Cheryl's Tip:
Separate the plain printed pages from those with nice photos, maps, or illustrations. Save these for the important areas of the boxes, such as the tops and fronts. Use the index for lining the insides of the boxes, since those are usually kind of plain.

Materials:

Assorted boxes in various sizes, with or without lids
An old book or other paper for covering
Plaid® Mod Podge, matte finish
1" foam brush
Matte spray sealer

3/4" satin ribbon or trim of choice
White glue
Razor blade or trimming knife

1 Using the razor blade or knife, remove the pages from the book. Discard the cover.

2 Working one side at a time, cover the surface of the box with the Mod Podge using the foam brush. Place the paper over the Mod Podge and brush the surface of the paper. Trim paper to fit.

3 After covering the entire box, inside and out, allow it to dry overnight.

4 Brush the outer and inner surfaces with two more coats of the Mod Podge, allowing it to dry between coats. Let the pieces dry thoroughly.

5 Spray the inside and outside of the box with the spray sealer. Allow the sealer to dry.

6 Cut the ribbon to fit around the box. Glue in place with the white glue. Tie a length of ribbon into a bow and glue to the box to finish the project.

Painted Wood Cheese Stand and Candleholders

I found the cake stand and the candleholders in different stalls at a flea market. The price for each was $1.99. They were ugly 1970s pieces with a dark finish but, as with everything else, I knew they had potential. The glass cheese dome came from the thrift store and cost 99¢. The grand total was a mere $4.97 for everything.

Cheese domes often contain some type of advertising or other writing. It can be easily removed with some nail polish remover and elbow grease.

Because the cake stand was really too small for normal use, I decided to use it as a cheese plate. Isn't it fun to see seemingly unrelated objects come together like this? I now use this set at many gatherings.

Cheryl's Tip: *Don't set food directly on the surface. Instead, place food on a clear glass plate as a "liner."*

Materials:

Small wooden cake stand
Soap and water
Set of wooden candleholders
Glass cheese dome

Medium and fine sandpaper
Satin finish spray paint in ivory
Satin finish spray sealer

1 Thoroughly clean and dry the items. Sand lightly with the fine sandpaper to remove any old wax or soap buildup. Wipe clean.

2 Spray the wooden items with two coats of spray paint and let them dry.

3 Using the medium sandpaper, lightly sand along all of the hard edges to reveal a bit of the old finish underneath. Using the fine sandpaper, do the same on the flat surfaces. Wipe clean.

4 Seal the items using two coats of the spray sealer; allow to dry thoroughly before using.

A Milk Maid's Centerpiece

Not all junk projects need to be labor-intensive. Some can be just plain fun. This project is a great example. I couldn't pass up this old wire milk-bottle caddy. It was in great shape and had to be useful for something! After rummaging in the cupboards, I found the sections were the perfect size for canning jars. A little water, some wild flowers, and a rustic raffia bow finish the look.

Cheryl's Tip:
Instead of placing flowers in the jars, use the piece as a condiment and cutlery caddy or a beverage server during your next outdoor barbecue.

Materials:

Milk bottle caddy
Soap and water
Cream-colored spray paint

Canning jars, milk bottles, or tall glasses
Raffia

1 Thoroughly clean the caddy using soap and water. Let it dry.

2 Paint the caddy using the spray paint. Allow the paint to dry.

3 Insert the jars into the caddy, and add what suits you.

4 Tie a raffia bow to the handle.

Salvage Yard Coat Rack

Check out your local architectural salvage yards for interesting finds that can be transformed into fun objects. I found this nifty old wooden item that used to sit atop an old Victorian-style door. A search through boxes of hardware at the same salvage yard yielded the hooks. Total cost of the coat rack was less than $10.

Cheryl's Tip:
Don't feel like you have to strip and repaint every item you find. The peeling paint gives this piece its charm!

M a t e r i a l s :

Chunk of architectural salvage, any size
Soap and water
Sandpaper
Rags
Brass hooks and screws
Two screw eyes
Picture wire

Nails
Pencil
Ruler
Hammer
Stud-finder
Level

1 Thoroughly clean the piece with soap and water—items from a salvage yard are often filthy from years of accumulation of dust and dirt.

2 Lightly sand the piece to remove anything that will snag your garments. Wipe the dust from the item with a clean rag.

3 Mark where you want to place your brass hooks. Space them at least 8" apart to allow for heavy coats to hang without crowding. Attach the hooks with screws.

4 On the back of the item, insert a screw eye 1" from each upper corner. Secure the wire to one screw eye securely. Thread the picture wire through the second screw eye and pull taut. Secure the wire to the second screw eye.

5 In most modern homes, studs are spaced 16" apart, but you can use the stud-finder to check. The idea is to make sure your coat rack can bear the weight of whatever you hang on it without harming the plaster or drywall. Hammer a sturdy nail into two wall studs, making sure the nails are level. Hang the wire over both nails to keep the coat rack from shifting.

Ivy-covered Side Chair

This gorgeous chair was literally a hunk o' junk when I found it beside the road. The tired, old piece had been put out with the trash. What a lucky find!

The previous owner watched from the window, shaking her head as I loaded the item into the back of my SUV—and dropped the loose chair seat on my toe. I swallowed my pride, picked up the seat, and tossed it into the back with the rest of the day's booty, which included this cute little side table.

When I arrived back home, the first items I decided to tackle were the chair and table. I knew they had potential!

Materials:

Old chair
Wood glue
DecoArt multi-purpose sealer
Americana® Satins acrylic paint (wide-mouth jar) in Soft White
DecoArt Americana acrylic paints in Sable Brown, Olive Green, Avocado, and Forest Green
DecoArt Faux glazing medium

Decorative fabric, about 20" x 20"
Muslin, about 20" x 20"
2 pieces heavy-weight quilt batting, about 20" x 20"
Fine sandpaper
Screwdrivers
Staple gun and staples
Assorted paintbrushes
Scissors

1 Remove the chair seat from the chair. Strip the chair seat down to the bare wood, discarding everything else. Using the seat base as a pattern,

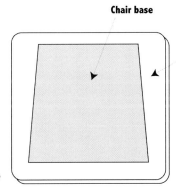

Chair base

2 layers of batting

cut the two pieces of batting to fit.

2 Wrap the muslin around the seat base, enclosing the batting. Trim the muslin to within 2" of the edges and staple the muslin in place on the seat bottom. Repeat with the decorative fabric. Set the chair seat aside.

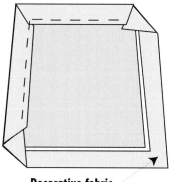

Decorative fabric

3 Re-glue any loose joints on the chair or table and allow the glue to dry. Sand both lightly with the sandpaper. Wipe clean.

4 Brush on the sealer and allow it to dry. Sand again lightly. Wipe clean.

5 Paint the chair and table with two coats of the satin acrylic paint, allowing the paint to dry between coats.

6 Using the Avocado acrylic paint slightly thinned with water and a fine-tipped brush, freehand the vines on all surfaces of the chair and table; you can paint as few or as many vines as you desire. Paint the leaves freehand, using various shades of the green paint. Let everything dry overnight.

7 Lightly sand both pieces again to give them a worn appearance. Wipe clean.

8 Mix equal parts of the brown acrylic paint with the glazing medium. Brush this glaze over the entire surface of the chair and table, wiping off the excess with a soft cloth. Allow the glaze to pool slightly at joints and in the sanded areas to give an antiqued appearance. Allow the glaze to dry.

9 Seal both pieces using the sealer, and allow to dry.

10 Reattach the chair seat and enjoy!

CHAPTER 3

Fresh Accents

Dashing Drum Table

I found this nifty table in a junk store. The leather top was in terrible shape, but the table had nice lines and was sturdy. I knew it only needed a little love and attention to bring it back to life.

Cheryl's Tip:
If you don't have leftover paint lying around, you can use acrylic craft paints.

Materials:

Wooden drum table
Medium sandpaper
Latex interior paints in tan and brown (I used leftover paints from the garage)
Delta Ceramcoat® Crackle Medium
Delta Ceramcoat® Exterior/Interior Varnish, matte finish

A length of artificial ivy
Tacky glue
Delta Ceramcoat® acrylic paint in Village Green and Wedgwood Green
Assorted paintbrushes
Waxed paper
Iron

1 Sand the entire surface of the table with medium sandpaper to remove any old wax buildup. If the top is ruined, sand it off. Wipe clean.

2 Paint the entire table using the tan paint and let it dry. It may take several coats; let each coat dry before applying the next one.

3 Paint the band around the sides of the table using the brown paint and let it dry. Apply the crackle medium generously over the brown paint and let dry (one to several hours, depending on temperature and humidity). Don't be in a rush; the medium needs to be completely dry.

4 Stroking in only one direction, apply the Tan paint to the sides. The item will crackle in the direction you stroke. Do not reapply over previously coated areas, or you could ruin the crackle. Allow the item to dry thoroughly.

5 Peel the ivy leaves from their plastic stems and press them flat with a warm iron. Using the tacky glue, affix the leaves in a random, rambling pattern over the surface of the table and on the leg. Cover the table with a layer of waxed paper and weight it down with some heavy books. This will help the leaves adhere to the table and dry perfectly flat. Let the glue dry for 48 hours.

6 Using a fine brush, paint the stems and tendrils freehand with the two shades of green craft paint. Let the paint dry overnight.

7 Seal the table with two coats of the matte varnish, allowing it to dry completely between coats.

Vintage Bathroom Shelf

This pretty little shelf, with a built-in towel holder, was one of my thrift store finds. I loved the shape and the pierced edgings—but not the accumulation of dust and grime, or the gaudy gold spray paint.

I took the item home and scrubbed it thoroughly. Afterwards, I stared at it for weeks wondering why on earth I even brought the thing home ... I was having second thoughts. After sanding some of the thick areas and age-old paint drips, I gave it a fresh coat of paint. It was starting to look better! After hanging it in my bathroom, I still wasn't satisfied, and was soon adding green accents. *Voila*—just what I wanted!

Cheryl's Tip:
The elegant glass canisters came from an outlet store, and are a great way to store and display necessary bath items such as soaps, swabs, and cotton balls. The vintage hand towel hanging from the towel bar is a charming addition.

Materials:

Vintage metal shelf
Soap and water
Medium and fine sandpaper
Satin finish spray paint in ivory or white

Paper plate
Acrylic craft paint in any color (I used
    sage green)
Small chunk of sea sponge

1 Sand any areas of thick paint build-up or dried drips with the medium sandpaper. Follow up with the fine sandpaper to smooth the surface.

2 Clean and dry the shelf well. Make any necessary repairs on the shelf.

3 Spray with two coats of the spray paint, and let it thoroughly dry.

4 Squeeze a small amount of the acrylic craft paint on a paper plate. Using the sea sponge, lightly dab the paint all over the surface of the shelf, allowing some of the white paint to show through it. Allow the shelf to dry.

5 Hang (see step 5 on page 33) and enjoy.

Canning Jar Candleholders

If you rummage through your kitchen, chances are you'll come across a few canning jars. If not, you can find them at nearly every garage sale or flea market. For just $5, I bought a box of jars so huge, my husband had to carry it to the car. I came away with about 30 quart-size jars—I was so thrilled with my find that I did the happy-dance right there in the street.

I've trimmed the jars with a plaid fabric to coordinate with the room setting, but you can easily substitute any fabric or color. You may even decide to trim the jars with raffia or pretty ribbon.

Cheryl's Tip:
These candleholders are not airtight. Don't put anything in the jars that you intend to use eventually, because it will go stale.

Materials:

- One-quart canning jar with standard opening—don't use wide-mouthed jars
- Soap and water
- Beans, pasta, rice, or other filler
- Small glass candle cup
- Votive candle
- One 2" x 30" strip of plaid woven fabric

1 Clean the jar in hot soapy water and rinse well. Dry to a sparkle.

2 Fill the jar to within 1" of the top with your filler.

3 Place the candle cup into the opening, wiggling it a bit to seat it in the filler. Insert the votive candle.

4 Fray the edges of the fabric a bit by pulling on loose threads. Tie the length of fabric into a bow around the neck of the jar to finish the project.

Hanging Keepsake Box

Next time you buy soaps or a food gift packed in a wooden box, save the box! While such an item may seem next-to-worthless at first glance, it can become a real gem! If you don't happen to have a plain wooden box lying around, you can find similar boxes at craft supply stores.

The pretty trim on this project comes from a rather unlikely source—drawer knob facings. I found a bag of old cabinet hardware at an estate sale, and thought it would be interesting to see what I could do with the pieces. Some paint and a few decorative brass tacks later, and I have a perfect way to display an old brooch.

Cheryl's Tip:
An old pocket watch or pendant would also look beautiful displayed in this box.

M a t e r i a l s :

Small wooden box, approximately 7" x 8"
Spray primer, white
Americana® Satins acrylic paint (wide-mouth jar) in Soft White
DecoArt Americana acrylic paint in Sable Brown
4 brass drawer pull facings
9 decorative brass tacks
Tacky glue

Picture hanging hook and nail
Self-leveling picture hanger
Something pretty to hang in the box
Fine sandpaper
Hammer
Wire cutters
Assorted paintbrushes

1 Lightly sand the interior and exterior of the box. Wipe away the dust.

2 Referring to the diagram, glue the drawer pull facings to the outside edges of the box. Insert one of the tacks into the center of each facing, covering the hole. Insert a tack into each corner of the wooden box. Attach the picture hook to the inside of the box. Cut the spike off the remaining tack and glue the head of the tack to the top of the hook.

3 Spray interior and exterior with the primer and let the primer dry.

4 Paint the entire box, inside and out, with two coats of the soft white paint, allowing the paint to dry between coats. Let the box dry thoroughly.

5 Lightly sand the edges of the box to reveal a bit of the wood underneath. Wipe clean. Dilute a small amount of the sable brown paint with an equal amount of water. Using a soft cloth or paper towel, antique the box by wiping the thinned paint over the surface. Allow the brown paint to discolor the wood areas exposed during sanding, and to pool slightly in the nooks and crannies in the hardware. Wipe off the excess until you have the desired amount of antiquing. Let the box dry overnight.

6 Attach the self-leveling hanger to the back of the box and hang where desired. Place the pretty item on the hook inside the box.

It's a Frame-up! Bulletin Board

I'm always on the lookout for old frames. They can be handy for so many different things! I've turned them into trays and tables, and have used old frames for new art. When you see frames at flea markets and tag sales, I urge you to grab them!

Because of the generous proportions, I chose to transform this frame into a bulletin board for the office. It's just the right size to hang behind the desk for all those small bits of paper that you don't want to lose.

Cheryl's Tip:
Try cutting and gluing a piece of cork to the inside of a pretty tray for another nifty bulletin board idea!

M a t e r i a l s :

One old frame
Foam-core board, 1/4" thick to fit inside frame opening

Sheet of cork to fit inside frame opening
Tacky glue

1 Thoroughly clean the frame.

2 Glue the cork securely to the foam-core board, and allow the glue to dry.

3 Glue the corkboard inside the frame and allow the glue to dry before hanging (see step 5 on page 33) and using.

Tick-tock, a Painted Clock

I was helping my mother clean some of her kitchen cabinets one day and noticed an overabundance of pie tins. Seems she's been saving them since before I was born! I figured they had to be useful for something. For weeks, they sat on a shelf in my office as I debated about what to do with them. After a walk through the crafts store, I decided to transform one of them into a clock.

Cheryl's Tip:
If you're unable to locate small tin stars, you can substitute buttons or small wooden items.

M a t e r i a l s :

9" or 10" tin pie plate
1-1/2" tin stars, 4
Walnut Hollow Quartz Clock Movement
    for 1/4"-thick surfaces
Tacky glue

DecoArt™ No-Prep Metal Paint in Bright
    White, Real Red, Deep Blue, and
    Bright Gold
Assorted paintbrushes or foam brushes
Electric drill with 3/8" bit

1 Paint the stars using the gold paint and set them aside to dry. Paint the numerals on each star using a narrow brush and the red paint.

2 Drill a 3/8" hole through the center of the pie plate.

3 Paint the exterior of the pie plate with the blue paint using a wide brush and allow it to dry. Paint the interior bottom and the outer rim of the plate with the blue and allow it to dry. Paint the interior

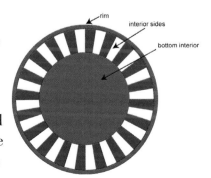

sides of the pie plate with the white paint. Let it dry. Using the white paint and a wide brush (about 1/2" wide), paint the red stripes. Let the paint dry.

4 Using the gold paint and a narrow, pointed brush, paint a squiggled line through the center of each red stripe. Paint a double line of gold on the plate rim above each white stripe.

5 Glue the gold stars in their proper positions inside the pie plate.

6 Following the manufacturer's directions, thread the clock unit through the hole in the pie plate and secure it in place. The clock movement includes a hanging hole, so be sure this points upwards on the back of the clock.

Painted Metal Cake Dome

Back in the '30s and '40s, aluminum was chic! You can find many aluminum items at flea markets and estate sales. This one had a horrible, black plastic knob, which I replaced with a vintage porcelain knob.

Metal items such as this are often a wee bit worn, so you'll have to knock out a few dents and dings with the rounded end of a hammer. Be gentle; it doesn't require much pressure to bend this metal back into shape.

Aluminum domes may not look like much in their original form, but with a little paint, you can transform them into really nifty décor pieces! I have several of these domes, each painted for a different season.

Cheryl's Tip:
Don't place food directly on the painted surface. Use a glass plate as a liner. This will protect the painted surface, and prevent contamination of food by paint.

Materials:

Aluminum cake dome with plate
DecoArt™ No-Prep Metal Paint in Bright Yellow, Sunlight Yellow, Sedona Clay, Ivory, Bright Blue, Strawberry Shake, Deep Fuchsia, Bright Lime Green, True Green, Fresh Lavender, Deep Purple

Soap and water
Saral transfer paper
Pencil
Small knob, if you wish to replace the original
Assorted paintbrushes

1 Clean and dry the dome and plate. Transfer the flower pattern to the outside of the cake dome using a pencil and the transfer paper, spacing the flowers 1" from the bottom edge.

2 Referring to the diagram, paint the sides of the cake dome. Paint a strip of Bright Lime Green to indicate the grass area. The pink dotted border directly beneath the green band is to be painted on the lip of the dome.

Paint the smaller flowers using the darker yellow paint on the left side and the lighter yellow paint on the right side. Highlight the darker side with lighter paint, and paint the accents on the lighter side with the darker paint. Repeat with the larger flowers using the pinkish shades of paint.

Paint the leaves, using darker green at each end of the leaves and lighter green in the centers. The stems are painted using only the darker green.

Paint the highlights around each flower using the Ivory paint.

3 Paint the top of the cake dome freehand. If the top has a wider or narrower circle than the one in the sample, you can adjust the size of the circle to suit your own dome. Add fuchsia dots to the pink center area.

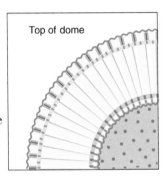

Top of dome

4 Paint the cake plate freehand, referring to the diagram. The blue dotted border is to be painted on the lip of the plate.

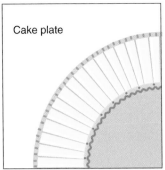

Cake plate

5 Let the paint dry for approximately 10 days before placing the dome on the plate and before using the cake dome.

CHAPTER 4

Gorgeous Gifts

Tea Tray Trends

Teapots and kettles without lids are a common site at thrift stores. They're overlooked by most buyers due to their sad demise, and can often be picked up for less than $2.00, depending on size and condition. Trays are also very common. A pretty teacup and saucer might require some hunting, but it's perfectly okay to buy, or put together, mismatched pieces.

I've used small pots of herbs in this kettle to carry through the "herbal tea" theme. If you prefer, the set would also look lovely planted with miniature roses, African violets, a small fern, or other small plant.

The entire tray, presented to a friend, makes a memorable birthday or get-well gift. Don't worry about everything matching—the eclectic mix is part of the charm of this grouping.

Cheryl's Tip:

If you have a lid for the teapot, you can set it to the side of the pot on the tray or tie it to the handle with pretty ribbon.

Materials:

Teapot or kettle
Metal polish
Rag
Soap and water
Small stones or marbles
Potted herbs

Potting soil
Tray, about 16" in diameter
Teacup and saucer
Tea bags
Spoon
Fancy ribbon

1 If the tray or spoon is tarnished, polish it with a cleaner made for that particular type of metal. Thoroughly clean everything in hot, soapy water. Rinse well, and dry.

2 Place a layer of stones or marbles inside the teapot or kettle. These will keep the roots of the herbs out of standing water, since the pot will not have drainage holes.

3 Fill the teapot or kettle half-full of potting soil. Remove the herbs from their pots and insert them into the pot. Fill the remaining open area of the teapot or kettle with potting soil, using your fingers or a spoon. Water just until moist.

4 Tie some pretty ribbon around the handle of the teapot or kettle.

5 Arrange everything on the tray and enjoy.

Elegant Glass Cake Plate and Dome

All of the items used in this project came from the flea market. I found a single glass candleholder with a solid base at one stall, and the dome and plate at another. A thorough cleaning and some clear household cement was all I needed to turn the items into a great cake stand. You can use it as a fabulous way to present a cake to a friend—or as a gift for yourself.

Cheryl's Tip:
When you come across these large domes during your junking sprees, bring them home. They can be hard to find!

Materials:

Glass candleholder with a wide base
Large glass plate
Large glass dome
Soap and water

Clear household cement such as E6000
Rubbing alcohol and a cotton ball
1" masking tape

1 Thoroughly clean and dry the items. Wet the cotton ball with the rubbing alcohol, and use it to clean the top rim of the candleholder and the bottom center of the plate. Let the bottom of the plate air-dry.

2 Turn the plate upside down on a level surface. Place a ring of glue the same size as the top rim of the candleholder in the center of the plate back. Turn the candleholder upside down, and set it on the plate directly on the glue.

3 Tape the candleholder in place so it won't slip and slide on the glue. Let the glue dry at least 48 hours before disturbing the tape.

4 Peel off the tape and turn the cake plate right side up. Set the glass dome atop of the plate and you're finished.

Guest Baskets

Pamper your overnight guests with a pretty basket filled with necessities they may have missed packing. It will be a much-appreciated addition to your guest bath.

Baskets such as this one are relatively easy to find at tag sales, but you can also find them at crafts stores. They're very inexpensive, so pick up a few of them and make several baskets. The fillings for the baskets can be found at most dollar stores and include toothbrushes, sample-sizes of toothpaste, lotions, powder, and other toiletries, a comb or brush, washcloths, and a nice bar of soap.

Hang the basket on the door of the guest room or place it near the sink in the guest bath so your guests will know it is meant for their use.

Cheryl's Tip:

Instead of a guest basket, you can adapt the idea for just about anything. For example, you can put together a winter-warmer basket with mittens, matching scarf, and packets of cocoa with a mug, or a new baby basket filled with baby oil, wipes, and diapers.

Materials:

Basket with handle
Two washcloths in any color

Assorted toiletries and other items (see above)
Several lengths of fancy ribbon

1 Line the bottom of the basket with one of the washcloths. Fold the second washcloth in thirds and stand it up toward the rear of the basket.

2 Arrange the toiletries and other items in the basket. Place the taller items toward the rear and the smaller items to the front.

3 Tie an assortment of pretty ribbons to the handle.

4 Set the basket out for your guests to enjoy.

Silver Plated Coaster Keepsake Ornament

You can often find solitary silver plate coasters at thrift shops, and they are in remarkably good condition. All they need is a little polishing. Collect enough of them and you can fill a tree!

Choose your favorite family photos for the centers. This one features my younger brother and me as "young-uns'."

Cheryl's Tip: *Little snippets of lace or old jewelry also look great in the centers of these ornaments.*

Materials:

Silver plate coaster, about 4" in diameter
Metal cleaner
Tacky glue

16" length of plaid satin ribbon
Hand-held electric drill with 3/8" bit

1 Scrub and polish the coaster.

2 Using the drill, make a hole in the rim of the coaster for threading the ribbon.

3 Scan and print, photocopy, or use a favorite original photo. Cut the photo to fit the center of the coaster. Glue the photo in place.

4 Fold the ribbon in half and thread it through the hole at the fold, from front to back, until you have about 1" of it pulled through at the back. Bring the doubled ends of the ribbon through the resulting loop and pull taut.

5 Tie the doubled ends of the ribbon into a bow and hang.

Teacup Gardens

Use your favorite teacups to make a temporary indoor garden by filling them with florist's foam and planting artificial flowers. Be sure to purchase good-quality artificial flowers for these projects. The goal is to have a realistic look—not the look of dime store phonies! Also, choose flowers that are smaller in scale in their natural state, such as violets, azalea, lily-of-the-valley, pansies, or African violets.

M a t e r i a l s :

Teacup with saucer
Chunk of florist foam cut to fit inside
   teacup
Florist putty
Dried green moss

Artificial flowers, 1 or 2 bunches
Small bunch of miniature trailing ivy
Hot glue gun and clear glue
Craft knife

1 Secure the cup on the saucer using a bit of the putty.

Putty

2 Trim the chunk of foam with a craft knife so it fits snuggly inside the teacup, having the top of the foam about 1/2" lower than the rim of the cup as shown.

1/2 inch from cup rim

3 Secure the foam in the cup using a lump of florist putty (do not glue it in place—florist putty will allow you to take the arrangement apart and re-use the cup later, if desired).

4 Using the hot glue gun, glue the moss to the top of the chunk of foam, being careful not to get any glue on the cup.

5 Insert the bunch of artificial flowers. If the plant seems too high for the cup, remove it and cut the stems to the proper size—*proportion* is important here—if the flowers are too tall, the arrangement will look unnatural and may topple over with the slightest breeze. Once the stems have been cut to the desired size, hot glue the stems in place in the foam.

6 Cut a few sprigs of ivy from the bunch and poke them into the foam as if they are trailing from the cup. Glue them in place.

7 Put the arrangement in a special spot to enjoy.

It's a Wrap

They look like old-fashioned Christmas crackers, but were made on-the-cheap from items found around the house, plus one less-than-glamorous item—toilet paper tubes. They're the perfect size for presenting small gifts. Use them at the table as place cards, or tuck them into the tree or secure them to a fresh wreath to add an unexpected touch.

You can also adapt the wrap for Hanukkah (as shown) or for birthdays and bridal showers. These little treasure-tubes make great party favors, too!

Cheryl's Tip:
You can also use paper towel tubes cut to size.

Materials:

Cardboard tube
Wrapping paper
Clear tape
Curling ribbon

Foil stickers or seals
Small gifts to tuck inside
Small white hangtags (optional)
Scissors

1 Clean off any paper that may still be clinging to the tube. Cut a 6" x 10" rectangle of wrapping paper.

2 Center the tube lengthwise of the rectangle of wrapping paper. Overlap the ends of the paper to enclose the tube and secure with a small piece of tape.

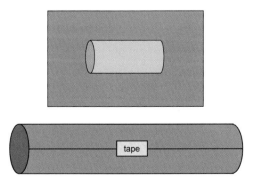

3 Cut two 12" lengths of curling ribbon. Gather one of the ends of the wrapping paper extending from the ends of the tube and tie the ribbon around it. Insert the gift into the open end and tie it off too. Curl the ribbon with scissors.

4 Affix a sticker or seal directly over the tape to conceal it.

5 Write the recipient's name on the hangtag and tie to one of the gathered ends.

Bottle Necklaces

A bag full of cabinet hardware purchased for $2.00 at a tag sale and a box of corks yielded the supplies and the inspiration for this project. Quick and easy to make, you'll have a set ready to use in about two hours.

Because you'll be writing on the corks, select ones that have no decoration on them. If you can't find any, you can remove the decorations on the cork by rubbing them with a piece of medium-grit sandpaper (also a great way to correct any mistakes you might make when writing the desired name on the label).

The glass bottles seen in the photograph are more of my lucky finds. I purchased them in different shapes and sizes for just $1 each at junk stores. The tray was something I happened to have laying around and thought it would make a terrific display for both bottles and necklaces. Cost of the entire vignette: less than $15.

Cheryl's Tip:
Before storing beverages or spirits in any glass bottle, check it for lead content using a home testing kit. You can find these kits at most markets and home-improvement centers.

M a t e r i a l s :

Flat faceplate (cabinet hardware)
10mm wooden beads (one natural, one brown), 2
12" length of hemp cording
Unmarked wine cork

Tube of silicon-based glue, such as E6000
Sharpie fine-point marking pen
Clear tape
Craft knife

1 Slice the wine cork in half lengthwise. Save the second half for an additional bottle necklace.

2 Fold the length of hemp cording in half and knot the end. Slip the beads over the folded end of the cording, positioning them about halfway from the knot.

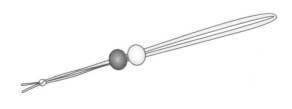

3 Glue the hemp loop to the back (wrong side) of the faceplate, centering the knot in the center of the piece of hardware. Place a piece of tape over the knot to secure it in place while the glue dries.

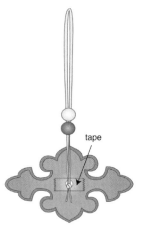

4 Using the Sharpie pen, write the desired information on the rounded side of the cork. The labels shown here include Gin, Scotch, Vodka, Sherry, Wine, Bourbon, Whiskey, Brandy, Cognac, and Water.

5 Glue the flat side of the cork to the front of the faceplate. Allow the glue to dry and remove the piece of tape. Slide the beads down the cord so they rest just above the faceplate before using the finished bottle necklaces.

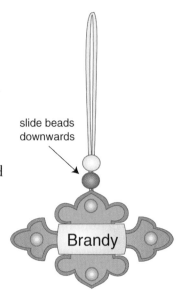

Recycled Romance

Using Vintage Textiles

Old embroidered textiles are fun to collect and use. Examples such as these from the '30s and '40s are readily available and still affordably priced. You can find them at estate sales, flea markets, and some garage sales.

Often you will come across sets of linens that are missing some of the pieces, one lonely but beautiful napkin, or others that are too worn to use for their original intent. These are the pieces I like best because they're very inexpensive—and it's fun to try to come up with ways to make them useful.

For these projects, I have used vintage linens that have been cleaned, pressed, and stitched to ready-made pillows. By tacking them in place in this manner, you can easily remove the linens and use them elsewhere if you desire. Runners can be wrapped around the pillows for a chic "envelope" look.

Materials:

Ready-made pillows, any size
Clean, pressed vintage textiles
All-purpose sewing thread

Hand sewing needle
Pins

1 Arrange the linens on the ready-made pillow. You can use a single item or multiple items; be creative. For the large pillow, I used a single embroidered doily and four crocheted drink coasters. The smaller pillow uses one dresser scarf.

2 Using the sewing thread and needle, hand-stitch the linens to the pillow front using small, hidden stitches. Use only enough stitching to hold the linens in place so you can easily remove them for cleaning or to change them later.

Romantic Beaded Candleholders

An assortment of candleholders in various shapes, sizes, and finishes can easily be refinished and refurbished for an elegant, pulled-together look. These were gathered from various places including yard sales, flea markets, and thrift stores.

These would make a lovely centerpiece for a bridal luncheon. If you can find enough smaller candleholders, have one at each place setting, reserving the largest one for the bride.

M a t e r i a l s :

Assorted metal candleholders
Soap and water
Off-white satin-finish metal spray paint
4mm ivory pearl beads, pre-strung
6mm ivory pearl beads
3mm gold beads, 1 package

Assorted sew-on jewels (they have a hole in each one), 1 package
24-gauge wire
Needle-nose pliers
Wire cutters
Electric drill, 1/8" bit

1 Thoroughly clean and dry each candleholder. Apply the spray paint.

2 Using the drill, make evenly-spaced holes around the top of the candleholder, directly over the legs, placing the hole 1/8" from the edges—or as close as you can comfortably get. The dash lines in the figure show the location of feet.

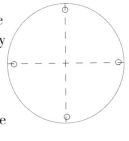

3 Cut a 10" length of wire for each hole. Fold wire in half and insert the folded end into each hole. String the beads between the wires, having an equal number of beads in each swag.

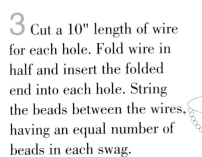

4 Place one 3mm gold bead on each wire. Feed the "legs" of the wire down through the holes using the needle-nose pliers.

5 Place another 3mm gold bead on the wire. String the jewels and additional beads or pearls on the wire as desired.

6 Place a final gold 3mm bead at the bottom of each decorative drop and feed the wires back up through several of the jewels. Clip off excess wire.

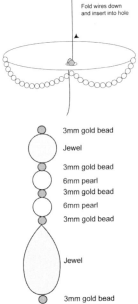

Fold wires down and insert into hole

3mm gold bead
Jewel
3mm gold bead
6mm pearl
3mm gold bead
6mm pearl
3mm gold bead

Jewel

3mm gold bead

Floral Vanity Stool

Vanity stools come in many shapes and styles, and are a common sight at thrift stores and tag sales. This one hails from about 1960, and was covered in an awful vinyl print. It was also very uncomfortable due to the lack of padding on the seat.

After spending half the day in the garage prepping and painting the piece, and the other half in the sewing room, the little stool has a fresh, new look, and a plump, comfy seat. While I chose to use a new floral fabric, the piece would look equally smashing clothed in vintage fabric.

Cheryl's Tip:
Use an electric knife to cut the foam quickly, evenly, and easily.

M a t e r i a l s :

Metal stool
Spray can of metal primer
Spray can of paint with suede finish in color of choice
Chunk of 3" foam slightly larger than the seat
1/2 yard of decorator fabric
3 yards of cording

Thread to match the fabric
Tube of silicon-based glue, such as E6000
Fabric glue
Sheet of fine sandpaper
Basic tools
T-pins
Serrated knife

1 Disassemble the stool, removing the top and any decorative components. Lightly sand the base. Wipe away any dust or residue. If the stool has removable feet, remove them.

2 Spray the base with the metal primer and allow it to dry. Spray the base with the paint and allow to dry.

3 Using the seat base as a pattern, trace the seat shape onto the piece of foam. Using a serrated knife, cut along the marked lines. Work slowly so you get a nice, smooth cut.

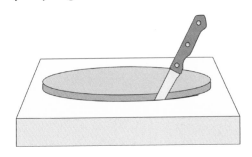

4 Using the seat base as a pattern, trace the seat pattern onto the wrong side of the fabric, centering any design elements. Add 1/4" seam allowances to the traced pattern and cut out along the outside line. Reassemble the stool.

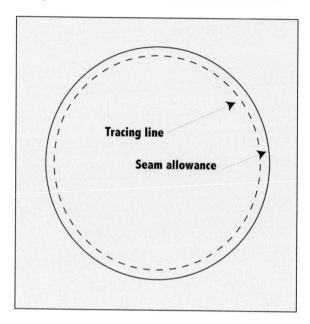

5 Cut a 4" wide strip of fabric long enough to completely go around the side of the seat plus 1/2". For example, if it takes 36" to go around the piece of foam, cut the strip 4" x 36-1/2". Glue the foam to the seat base, having the glue 1" from the edges of the base.

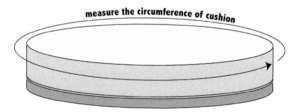

6 Stitch the short ends of the strip of fabric together, right sides facing, using a 1/4" seam allowance. Stitch the resulting short tube to the piece cut in step 4, using a 1/4" seam allowance.

7 Clip the curved edges of the seams close to, but not through, the seam line. This will make the curves nice and smooth. Turn the covering right side out and press along the seam lines. Place the covering over the foam—it should fit snugly. Tuck the bottom edges of the covering under the foam to conceal them, but don't glue yet.

8 To make the ruffle, cut a strip of fabric 6" wide and four times the circumference of the seat, piecing the fabric as necessary. Turn under 1/4" twice along one long edge and stitch close to the inside fold to hem. Stitch the two short ends of the strip together to form a short tube. Divide the tube into quarters and mark with a pin. Gather along the un-hemmed edge.

9 Using T-pins, arrange the ruffle around the seat, tucking it under the foam, making certain you evenly distribute the ruffles in each quadrant. Glue the ruffle to the seat base. Glue the tucked cover fabric to the seat base directly over the ruffle. This will conceal the raw edges of both the cover and the ruffle. Remove the T-pins.

10 Using fabric glue, glue the cording around the seam on the seat cover and around the area where the cover meats the ruffle. If you have extra cording left over, tie it into a bow and glue to the stool as a finishing touch.

Pretty Pansy Picture

Oh, the look of French plaster work! How lovely and delicate—only a true master can create such a work of art. Okay, okay—I admit it. The frame is plastic. It used to be an ugly, gold color, and it only cost 75¢ at a church sale. No one knows it, though, but me and you!

Materials:

Plastic frame
Ivory matte-finish spray paint
DecoArt™ Faux glazing medium
DecoArt™ acrylic paint, Sable Brown
Marbled, decorative paper, 1 piece
1/2" foam brush

Set of rub-on transfers featuring pansies
   or other flowers
Rags
Craft glue
Wide, wired edge ribbon in color of
   choice, 40"

1 Disassemble the frame and clean thoroughly. Reserve the glass and throw the rest of the "innards" away.

2 Paint with the ivory spray paint. It may take several coats to completely cover the frame. Make certain the paint penetrates into all the nooks and crannies. Allow the frame to dry completely.

3 Mix a small amount of the sable brown paint with a small amount of the glazing medium; one-to-one is a good ratio. Using the sponge, brush the glaze over the frame. Wipe off the excess immediately using the rag, allowing some of the glaze to penetrate into the nooks and crannies. Allow the glaze to dry completely.

4 Using the glass as a pattern, cut a new piece of cardboard for the backing. Glue the decorative paper to the cardboard shape and trim the paper to fit.

5 Following the manufacturer's directions, transfer the decals to the paper.

6 Reassemble the frame. Cut the ribbon into two 20" lengths. Using the first length, tie a bow around the second length and center it. Fold the long ends downward. Glue the long ends of the ribbon to the back of the frame and allow the glue to dry thoroughly before hanging.

Bridal Keepsake Box

This beautiful box began its life as a dark, wooden jewelry box with a cheesy faux-needlepoint padded top. Now it's a gorgeous place to keep bridal (or other) treasures. This box measures approximately 8" x 10" … the perfect size to keep on your night table or dresser.

Cheryl's Tip:
If you can't find artificial flowers you like, you can also use the materials from a floral garland or floral candle ring.

Materials:

DecoArt™ Americana® acrylic paint, Light Buttermilk and Sable Brown
DecoArt™ DuraClear™ interior varnish, satin finish
Assorted paintbrushes
Rag
Paper plate
Medium sandpaper

Decorative paper, 2 sheets 8-1/2" x 11"
Tacky glue
Assorted artificial flowers or greenery
Brass polish
Scissors
Craft knife
Tweezers

1 Using a sharp knife, cut out the padded top along the edge of the molding. Pull out any remaining bits of fabric from the lid with tweezers. Remove the hardware and set it aside.

2 Thoroughly clean and dry the box. Remove the innards using a knife. Sand off any remaining glue. Lightly sand the exterior and interior surfaces of the box to remove any wax accumulation. Wipe clean.

3 Paint the inside and outside of the box with two coats of Buttermilk paint, letting the paint dry thoroughly between coats. To simulate natural wear, sand the box again. Sand harder in some areas to reveal a small bit of the old finish underneath, especially at the corners and front of the box.

4 On a paper plate, squeeze out a small amount of the Sable Brown paint. Thin slightly with water. Using a rag, wipe the paint on the painted surface as you would a stain. Let it sit for a moment and wipe off the excess. Repeat until you have the desired amount of "antiquing." Let the brown paint dry.

5 Seal the exterior of the box with the varnish. Let dry.

6 Cut the paper to fit the bottom of the box. Coat the bottom of the box with glue and press the paper in place. Repeat with the inside sides and the inside lid area.

7 Cut the flowers from their stems and glue them to the top of the box lid. Hide any gaps by gluing some of the foliage from the stems in the gaps. Let the glue dry.

8 Clean the hardware with brass polish and reassemble the box.

Junk Jeans Throw and Pillows

My teenage daughters are really into blue jeans—and so am I. We wear them until they can't hold themselves together at the seams any longer. By that time though, they're worn to a soft, silky texture and a mellow blue hue. Perfect for projects!

Although there's actually quite a bit of fabric in a pair of jeans, you'll need about four pairs of teen-adult sized jeans to make the throw. If you want to make it larger, simply round up a few extra pairs and add more rows.

After stitching the throw, wash it several times in warm water and tumble dry. This will give the seams that nice, fluffy, worn look.

Cheryl's Tip:
If you prefer to make your own binding, old shirts work beautifully!

Materials:

4 pairs of teen or adult-size jeans
Medium blue all-purpose sewing thread
5 yds of extra-wide, double -old bias tape

14" pillow form for each pillow
Assorted embellishments such as
   patches, trims, or embroidery floss

1 Cut the legs from the jeans 2" below the pockets. Cut along the side and inseams—don't try to open the seams with a seam ripper because it's not worth the work. You'll have two pieces of fabric from each leg.

2 Cut 80 squares, 6" x 6", from the leg pieces.

3 Place two of the squares together having their wrong sides facing (the seams will be on the right side of the finished project). Using a 1/4" seam allowance and a tight stitch, sew the squares together. Repeat, stitching eight squares together to make a row.

4 Continue stitching eight squares together to make ten rows. Stitch the ten rows together.

5 Bind the edges of the throw.

6 To make each pillow, cut eight 7" squares of fabric. Stitch four of the squares together to make the pillow front, and four to make the pillow backing.

7 Cut out one pocket 1/4" from the pocket edges. Turn the raw edges towards the back of the pocket and baste them in place.

8 Stitch the pocket to the center of the four-square pillow front.

9 Embellish the throw and pillow fronts as desired using patches, trim, or embroidery.

10 Stitch the pillow front to the pillow backing, having their wrong sides facing and using a 1/4" seam allowance. Leave a 10" opening along the bottom edge. Insert the pillow form and stitch the bottom edge closed.

11 Wash and dry the items several times to fluff the seams.

Jeans Pocket Organizer

Don't throw away the pockets from the junk jeans throw and pillow project. Save them for making this handy wall organizer. It'll work beautifully in the bathroom, laundry room, kid's room, or kitchen and is, of course, machine washable.

Cheryl's Tip: *Make this project as long as you need it—you're only limited by the length of the leg of the pants.*

Materials:

One jeans leg, adult sized
6 or more pockets
Dowel or stick for hanging

Heavy-duty sewing thread in blue to match jeans
Twine or jute

1 Cut the jeans leg along the inseam (the one to the inside the leg). Cut off the bulky inseam area from the leg. Press flat.

2 Cut the leg to the length desired plus 1". For example, if you want the organizer to be 22" long like the sample, cut the length of the leg at 23".

3 Fold under 1/2" twice to the back of the leg on the cut bottom of the leg. Repeat with the sides. Stitch the doubled hem in place by machine using the heavy-duty thread.

4 Pin the jeans pocket to the leg. Stitch around the sides and bottom edges of the pockets, leaving the tops unstitched.

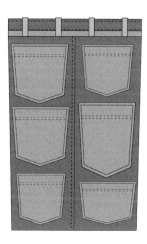

5 Hang the organizer by inserting a dowel or stick through the belt loops. Cut a 20" length of twine and tie to each end of the dowel or stick and hang.

Breakfast in Bed

A mismatched collection of white dishes was all I needed to create this French Provincial-inspired breakfast set. Every item on this tray was purchased someplace different and was made by a different manufacturer. It's the decoration that makes this a cohesive set.

The painting on this set is also done completely freehand, but don't let that scare you! Everything is painted using simple lines and dots—no fancy stroke-work, here.

Materials:

Assorted white ceramic dishes
Delta Ceramcoat® Perm Enamel™
    Surface Conditioner
Delta Ceramcoat® Perm Enamel™
    Paints in Celestial Blue, Citrus Yellow,
    Red Red, True Green, Limeade and
    Ultra White

Delta Ceramcoat® Perm
    Enamel™Thinner
Delta Ceramcoat® Perm Enamel™ Clear
    Gloss Glaze
Assorted paintbrushes
Paper plate
Soap and water

1 Thoroughly clean and dry each piece of dinnerware. Brush on the surface conditioner and allow it to dry—do not wipe the excess. The surface conditioner will help the paint bond with the silica in the dinnerware.

2 On a paper plate, squeeze out a small amount of the Citrus Yellow paint. Add two drops of the thinner, mix well, and paint a 2" diameter circle for the sun. Add two drops of the white paint to half of the yellow paint on the plate and mix well. Randomly paint the triangles radiating around the yellow circle using a small, pointed brush. Add the accent marks to the triangles in the brighter yellow using a very fine brush. Using a small brush with a rounded end, dab circles of the lighter yellow paint inside the sun circle.

5 Mix a small amount of the white paint with some blue paint to achieve a medium shade of blue—two parts blue to one part white is good. Mix well. You won't need to add the thinner to this mixture. Using a small brush with a rounded end, dab circle of blue randomly on the stem lines. Make several flowers consisting of five dots here and there.

3 Squeeze a small amount of the True Green paint on the paper plate and add two drops of the thinner. Mix well. Using the fine brush, paint the stem lines around the plate and saucer. Paint stems on the cup and bowl.

6 Make additional random dots using undiluted red paint. Dab a circle of red in the center of each five-dot flower. Dab the red paint, evenly spaced, around the rims of each piece of dinnerware.

7 Dilute the red paint with two drops of thinner. Paint the lettering on the cup.

8 Let everything dry thoroughly, and brush on the clear gloss glaze.

9 Let dry for at least 10 days to set the paint. After this time, it is safe to hand-wash the items.

4 Mix an equal amount of the True Green with the Limeade and add two drops of thinner. Mix well. Using a small pointed brush, paint leaves randomly along the stems.

CHAPTER 6

Creative Flourishes

Seaside Frames

Old photo frames are a common sight at any tag sale, flea market, or thrift store. Some are in less-than-perfect condition and sell for less than a dollar. By adding a fresh coat of paint and some embellishment, you can turn ordinary, mismatched frames into beautiful accents for your home in no time at all.

Cheryl's Tip:
I pilfered the glass stones from my mother's house (with her permission, of course). If you don't have glass stones on hand, you can also use marbles, buttons, polished rocks, sea glass, or assorted seashells.

Materials:

Old photo frame
Soap and water
Satin-finish white spray paint
Glass accent stones
Hot glue gun and clear glue

A pretty seashell
Medium sandpaper
All-purpose white glue
Small, old paintbrush
Beach sand

1 Remove the backing and glass from the frames. Lightly sand the frames and clean them thoroughly. Allow them to dry completely.

2 Spray the frame with the white spray paint and let it dry.

3 Using the glue gun, attach the seashell to the center top of the frame. Glue the glass accent stones around the perimeter of the frame.

4 Paint inbetween some of the glass stones with the glue and immediately sprinkle with sand. Wipe excess sand from the glass stones.

5 Clean and replace the glass. Insert photos and the backing and enjoy.

Decoupage Picnic Canisters

We all tend to have tins such as these lying around in closets and cupboards. Once upon a time, they were filled with such goodies as cookies, candy, and caramel corn. The goodies are long gone but we all think we'll have a need for the tins "some day."

Well everybody, "some day" is finally here! Transform those tins into canisters to keep your picnic goodies safe and fresh. If you can't locate any tins in your own abode, beg from the neighbors.

Cheryl's Tip:
For best results, choose tins that do not have embossed decorations in their lids or bodies—these will still be visible in the finished tins.

Materials:

Metal boxes with lids
Pretty gift wrap or decorative papers
Jute twine, ribbon, or desired trim
1"-wide foam brush

Plaid® Mod Podge®, matte finish
Spray sealer, matte or gloss
Razor blade or trimming knife

1 Cut a length of gift wrap or paper that will completely encircle the side of the can, fitting between the raised band at the bottom and the area that will be covered by the lid.

measure the circumference of can

distance between raised bands

2 Using the sponge brush, completely coat the outside of the can with the Mod Podge. Press the paper onto the can, smoothing out any large wrinkles. Small circles will remain, but most of these will disappear as the Mod Podge dries and the paper contracts.

3 Trace the lid onto the backside of the paper. Measure the side height of the lid and add this measurement to the circle. Cut out circle along the outer line.

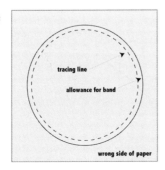

tracing line

allowance for band

wrong side of paper

4 Coat the tops and sides of the lid, and apply the paper as you did for the can. Using a razor blade or knife, trim the paper so that it lies within the raised lip of the lid.

5 Decorate the can with paper cutouts, gluing them in place using the Mod Podge.

6 Coat the can and lid with Mod Podge and allow them to dry. When they are completely dry, apply a second coat and allow the second coat to dry thoroughly—preferably overnight.

7 Glue the trim to the can as desired. Allow to dry.

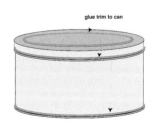

glue trim to can

8 Spray the outside of the can and lid with the sealer to finish.

Abscond with Some Sconces

These sconces were so cheap they seemed like a steal! I could see their potential immediately and brought them home, despite their tarnished condition. A dear friend fell in love with their shape, so after painting them I ended up giving them to her as an early birthday gift. She also got the botanical pictures ... I like to spoil my friends and family.

Cheryl's Tip:
You can use sconces made of any material, including plastic, wood, or metal.

Materials:

Pair of sconces
Metal cleaner
Soap and water
All-purpose spray primer
Mini artificial ivy

Krylon Make It Suede! Textured paint, Berber
DecoColor Broad Line Liquid Gold™ paint marker

1 Thoroughly clean the sconces. If they are metal, use a metal cleaner to remove any tarnish or finish. Wipe clean. Allow them to dry completely.

2 Spray the sconces with the primer and let them dry overnight.

3 Spray the sconces with the textured paint and allow them to dry thoroughly.

4 Using the marker, make a gold accent line around the edges of the sconce back and candle cup—and anywhere else on the sconce that you deem appropriate.

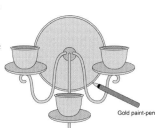

Gold paint-pen

5 Wind a few sprigs of the artificial ivy around the base of the sconce. Hang, insert candles, and enjoy.

Framed Botanicals

Here's a fun way to use a pile of dime-store frames. No one will ever know these "prints" cost you almost nothing to make.

Because many true botanical prints include the Latin name of the plant, you can add it to the background paper using your computer and printer. However, if you're too lazy to look up their true names, you can do what I did—make them up! Some of the names I chose include "Foundsum Fernicus" and "Notsure Whatitis." Be creative with your made-up names!

Also, if you don't have access to a computer and printer, you can draw the lettering freehand on your paper in any style or color you desire. Practice first on scratch paper until you achieve the desired look.

Cheryl's Tip:
Don't hang the botanicals in direct sunlight. They will eventually fade.

Materials:

8-1/2" x 11" gold-tone dime store "document" frame
8-1/2" x 11" piece of decorative paper
Pieces of pretty plants

Paper towels and heavy books
All-purpose glue
Computer and printer

1 Place the plants between two paper towels. Sandwich them between two big books for two weeks.

2 Select a pretty font on your computer and print the desired names of the plants at the bottom center of each piece of paper. Space the lettering about 1" from the center bottom.

Thinkits Pretty

3 Using small beads of glue, attach the pressed plants to the paper. The glass will help hold the plants in position.

4 Insert the paper into the frames, hang, and admire your handiwork.

Dainty Corner Shelf

I found this vintage corner shelf at a tag sale in an old part of town. The price tag said a mere buck-and-a-half. Naturally, I snapped it up before anyone else spotted it!

The poor old shelf was in need of some TLC. After re-gluing everything in place and sanding the surface, it was ready to decorate. Some paint and a decorative edging cut from pop cans was all it needed to complete its transformation from ugly duckling into beautiful swan.

Cheryl's Tip:
You can also build your own shelf. Plans are available on my Web site. See the references section in the back of the book.

Materials:

Vintage corner shelf
Spray can of primer
DecoArt™ Americana acrylic paint, Warm White and Pink Chiffon
2 clean, empty pop cans
Foam brush, 1" wide
#5 pointed round paintbrush
Tube of silicon-based glue, such as E6000

Fine sandpaper
Utility scissors
Hole punch
Stylus
Piece of craft foam
Cotton quilt batting, or other soft surface

1 If the shelf is loose, re-glue using wood glue, and allow to dry.

2 Spray the shelf with the primer and allow it to dry. Using the sponge brush, paint the shelf with the Warm White.

3 Mark vertical lines on shelf very lightly with a pencil, spacing them 1" apart. Paint along the lines using the pointed round brush and the Pink Chiffon. Using the sponge brush, paint the side edges of the shelf with the Pink Chiffon.

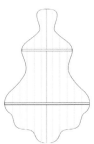

4 Cut the pop cans down the side using the utility scissors. Start at the hole and cut toward the bottom of the can. Cut around the top and discard. Repeat with the bottom. Flatten the resulting sheet of metal by rolling it the opposite direction.

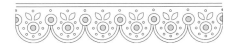

5 Trace as many repeats of the lace pattern as necessary to trim your shelf. Cut out and make the holes using the hole punch. Place the bands, painted side up, on the piece of craft foam. The painted side will be the wrong side of the band. The bare metal side is the right side.

6 Using the stylus, emboss the designs on the bands, pressing gently until the pattern shows up clearly on the opposite side of the strips.

7 Spray both sides of the metal bands with primer and allow it to dry. Sponge on the Warm White paint and allow it to dry.

8 Lightly sand on the embossed side to expose the bare metal.

9 Glue the lace bands to the shelf to finish the project.

Lively Log Candleholder

Here's a project for which you can scavenge! Check your woodpile—or your neighbor's woodpile—for just the right log. You'll know it when you see it. The best logs are 6" to 10" in length, and have a diameter of 5" to 7". Be sure to select logs with flat bottoms so they won't wobble.

Cheryl's Tip:
ALWAYS use a glass candle cup when burning candles in a flammable candleholder.

Materials:

One well-dried log with a flat top and bottom
Coarse sandpaper

Raffia
Glass candle cup and small votive candle
2" paddle bit and hand-held electric drill

1 Sand the upper and lower edges of the log to take some of the sharpness off the edges.

2 Using the drill bit, make a 1" deep hole in the center top of the log.

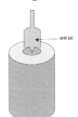

drill bit

3 Insert the candle cup into the hole and add the candle.

4 Tie a few lengths of raffia or jute around the candleholder and enjoy.

Vinyl Floor Cloth

Scraps of vinyl make great floor cloths! It doesn't matter what the style or pattern of the vinyl flooring is, because you paint on the wrong side of the vinyl. If you have cans of acrylic latex interior paint lying around, it can be used in place of the acrylic craft paint.

Cheryl's Tip:
You can get vinyl scraps from most flooring stores or construction sites. Don't use flooring that has been previously installed because you need a smooth backside.

Materials:

Scrap of vinyl flooring
Delta Ceramcoat® acrylic paint, in assorted colors
Spray sealer, matte

Assorted paintbrushes
Paper plates
Pencil
Ruler

1 Cut the vinyl flooring to the desired size. Mark the borders in the desired width with a pencil and ruler.

2 Using the pencil, draw the leaves or other decoration freehand. Your art need not be perfect.

3 Squeeze some of the acrylic paint onto the paper plate. Paint the background area and the borders using the assorted paintbrushes. Let the paint dry completely.

4 Paint the leaves or other decoration. Let the paint dry overnight.

5 Seal the floor cloth with two coats of sealer, allowing each coat to dry between applications.

Gettin' Twiggy with It

The lodge-look is popular and easy! Search through the house for items you may already have on hand and transform them into rustic accessories using nothing more than paint, glue, and items from the great outdoors.

After a quick search of the garage and crafts storage in my office, I came up with a switch plate, photo frame, door hanger, and plaque, and some old pieces of fishing tackle. Other suitable items can include wooden and metal storage containers, boxes, trays, and even a lamp base.

Materials:

Clean, paintable surface, such as those
    shown in the photo
Fine sandpaper
Delta Ceramcoat® Crackle Medium
Delta Ceramcoat® acrylic paint in Light
    Ivory, Light Chocolate, Dark Burnt
    Umber, and Forest Green
Delta Ceramcoat® exterior/interior
    varnish, matte finish

Twigs, rocks, fishing tackle, dried plants
    and other lodge-related findings
Tacky glue or extra-strength adhesive
Paintbrushes
Chunk of sea sponge
Pruning shears
Graphite transfer paper
Screw eyes
Jute or twine

1 Lightly sand and clean the surface you are going to paint. Apply the base coat of the Light Chocolate acrylic paint and allow the paint to dry.

2 Apply the crackle medium generously and let dry; it could take from one to several hours depending on temperature and humidity. Don't be in a rush, because the medium needs to be completely dry!

3 Stroking in only one direction, apply the Light Ivory acrylic paint to the surface. The item will crackle in the direction you stroke. Do not reapply over previously coated areas or you could ruin the crackle. Allow the item to dry thoroughly.

4 If you are making the door hanger or sign, enlarge the patterns shown to the desired size, and transfer the lettering to the painted item using the transfer paper. Paint the lettering using the Forest Green acrylic paint.

5 Using a sponge, lightly dab the surface with the Dark Burnt Umber to give it a birch bark look. Use only a tiny amount of paint on your sponge—it needs to be almost dry for the proper effect.

6 Glue dried twigs to the painted surface. You can arrange them around the perimeter or in a decorative pattern. Refer to the photograph for inspiration.

7 Glue rocks, dried plants, fishing tackle, and other findings to the surface and allow to dry, preferably overnight.

8 Coat the entire surface with the varnish and allow it to dry.

9 Attach screw eyes to the sign or frames and hang using the jute twine.

CHAPTER 7

Secondhand Savvy

Mixing and Matching Dinnerware

During your junk-hunting adventures, you are going to come across a lot of dinnerware. You'll find everything from complete sets of vintage china to saucers and cups missing their mates.

I like to collect old china and mix-and-match table settings. It's great fun to see each guest sit down at his or her place and start comparing plates and accessories. It's a great way to start a conversation.

While collecting everything you see can be tempting, do try to collect with a purpose in mind. I like to develop a theme. For example, I have one box of treasures that features pink roses on every piece, and another box that features violets. Each item is completely different, but the theme ties them together. Sometimes I use an assortment of different china patterns on the table.

I also like to use plain glass items to further expand the theme or to fill in for items that I haven't yet uncovered in bone china. Glass goes well with everything!

I'm giving you some examples here by showing several of my favorite mix-and-match themes.

Cheryl's Tip:

Collect small glass vases to use at each place setting. Encourage your guests to take their little vase of flowers home with them as a souvenir of a wonderful evening.

Materials:

Assorted dinnerware in china, glass, and stoneware in assorted sizes

Assorted utensils

1 Thoroughly clean and dry the items. Set your table and enjoy.

Rose-Trimmed Napkin Rings

I found a bag full of brass napkin rings at an estate sale. Six of them actually matched; the rest were odds and ends.

They were in awful condition, even after a thorough polishing, so I decided to paint them. After painting, I thought they looked too plain, so I decorated them with ribbon roses. Now I actually like them! It's odd the way the creative process works.

Cheryl's Tip:
Wood or plastic napkin rings will also work just fine.

Materials:

Plain napkin rings
Satin finish spray paint in ivory or white
Acrylic craft paint in any color

Tacky glue
Small ribbon roses—3 per ring
Small paintbrushes

1 Remove the tarnish from the napkin rings if they are metal. Spray the napkin rings inside and out with the spray paint and let them dry.

2 Paint the lines on the napkin rings using the acrylic craft paint. Allow the paint to dry.

3 Glue three roses to the top of each napkin ring and let the glue dry. The rings are now ready for use.

Enticing Glass Accents

Back in our mothers' and grandmothers' heyday, homemakers had a different set of glassware for every drink known to mankind. Now that we live in the era of "all-purpose" goblets, many of these nifty-shaped glass items find their way into estate sales and thrift stores.

I like to collect sets of pretty-shaped glassware and use them as dessert glasses, such as these I've shown here. You can select from martini and champagne glasses or any other glass with a wide bowl. Set each glass on a pretty plate for a lovely presentation.

Cheryl's Tip:
If you find unadorned glassware, paint your own decorations on them.

M a t e r i a l s :

Champagne or martini glasses, any size
Soap and water

Saucer
Something yummy to put inside them

1 Thoroughly wash the glassware in hot, sudsy water. Rinse thoroughly and dry to a sparkle.

2 Place the glass on the saucer and fill. Present at the table.

More Enticing Glass Accents

I have a "thing" for glassware. I'm drawn to it like a moth to a flame. I can see the sparkle from across the room, or across the street, and zero in. Admittedly, I have enough glassware to make a new lens for the Hubble telescope.

A year or so ago, some friends and I decided to have a girls' day out to honor our friend, who had a hysterectomy a few weeks' beforehand. She was still hobbling around the house, afraid to move, so we decided to take her out for the day. After visiting a few local antique stores and swooning over the prices—or was it the heat—we ditched the antiques and headed for the thrift stores. We had a blast!

To make a long story short, I found three of these little glass leaves at one thrift store and *had* to have them—they were a mere 49¢ apiece. With my last name, Fall, collecting leaves makes perfect sense. We visited several more thrift and secondhand stores throughout the day, and I ended finding six leaves altogether. Now I have ten.

Originally, these glass items were intended as candy or bonbon dishes, but I use them as salad plates for my fall table. The gold accent adds elegance to the leaves.

Cheryl's Tip:
Hand-wash the plates after using them to avoid losing any of the gold banding.

Materials:

Glass bonbon plate
Soap and water
Rubbing alcohol and cotton balls

DecoColor Broad Line Liquid Gold™ paint marker

1 Thoroughly wash the glassware in hot, sudsy water. Rinse thoroughly and dry to a sparkle.

2 Dampen the cotton ball with the rubbing alcohol and clean the rim with the alcohol. Allow the rim to air-dry.

3 Paint a gold band around each leaf using the marker and let dry.

Romantic Painted Glassware

As you venture out into the world to find great junk, you'll come across a plenitude of glassware. It's a common site at every garage sale, flea market, and tag sale out there. It's a pity the sellers don't have better imaginations! With a little time and paint, humble glassware can be transformed into beautiful one-of-a-kind items that will rival the expensive stuff in the boutiques.

Simple brushstrokes make the project easy and satisfying. It's also a quick project to finish—but you will have to wait 10 days before using the glassware so the paint will have a chance to cure.

Materials:

Two glasses
Soap and water
Delta Ceramcoat® Perm Enamel™
    Surface Conditioner
Delta Ceramcoat® Perm Enamel™
    Paints in Cream, Sea Foam Green,
    and Crocus Yellow

Delta Ceramcoat® Perm Enamel™
    Thinner
Delta Ceramcoat® Perm Enamel™ White
    Frost Etched Glass Effect
Clear tape
Assorted paintbrushes
Paper plate

1 Thoroughly clean and dry each glass. Brush on the surface conditioner and allow it to dry; do not wipe the excess. The surface conditioner will help the paint bond with the silica in the dinnerware.

2 Brush the white frost solution around the top of each glass, making a 1/2" band. Brush the frost solution onto the base of the glass. Let dry overnight.

3 Trace the flower shape onto a small piece of paper. Cut out, and tape the shape to anywhere inside of a glass.

4 On a paper plate, squeeze out a small amount of the Cream paint. Add two drops of the thinner, mix well, and paint the flower, following the pattern taped to the inside of the glass. Paint four to five flowers on each glass. Add two drops of the white paint to 1/2 of the yellow paint on the plate and mix well. Using a small brush with a rounded end, dab circles of the yellow paint at the center of the flowers to make the flower centers.

5 Squeeze a small amount of the Sea Foam Green paint on the paper plate and add two drops of the thinner. Mix well. Using a very small, pointed brush, paint groups of leaves near the flowers. You can paint as few or as many as you desire. With a very fine brush, paint the stem lines.

6 Let dry for at least 10 days to set the paint. After this time, it is safe to hand-wash the items.

Dainty Cork Coasters

Make these pretty little cork coasters to match the glassware on the previous page or match them to something in your home. You can easily customize them by using something different in the centers of the coasters.

These coasters were found at a tag sale and actually had some funky art on them, which I didn't care for. The bottoms of the coasters were clean. I painted the ugly side so I wouldn't have to look at it ever again. If you prefer new coasters, you can find them in varying shapes and sizes at craft stores.

Cheryl's Tip:
Greeting card cutouts and scrapbooking stickers or cutouts make great centers for these coasters.

Materials:

Cork coasters
Plaid® Mod Podge® in matte finish
Delta Ceramcoat® Acrylic Paint, Light Ivory
Spray sealer, matte or gloss

2 packages Jolee's Boutique™ sticker collages from Stickopotamus®, Vanilla Flowers
Assorted paintbrushes

1 Paint the underside (formerly the icky side) and the sides of the coasters with the Light Ivory paint. Paint a 1/4" line around the edges of the top (cork side) of the coasters and let the paint dry thoroughly.

2 Using the Mod Podge and a small brush, adhere one large and one small flower to each coaster. Let the Mod Podge dry.

3 Coat the tops of each coaster with three layers of the Mod Podge, letting it dry between coats.

4 After the coasters have dried for several days (don't be in a rush), spray them with the sealer to protect the pretty surfaces.

Fantastic Finials

This great-looking accent piece has the look of an expensive architectural collectible. But it's actually constructed from a glass light shade, a wood circle, and a creative paint finish. You can find glass light shades at flea markets and secondhand stores, but if a prettily-shaped one such as this is elusive, try using a vase turned upside-down and glue an interesting piece of hardware or bric-a-brac to the end.

Materials:

Glass light shade
Soap and water
Round, beveled wood circle plaque
    slightly larger than the end of the
    glass shade
Modern Options Copper Topper™
    Metallic Surfacer

Modern Options Patina Green™
    Antiquing Solution
Delta Ceramcoat® acrylic paint, black
Tube of silicon-based glue such as
    E6000
Sandpaper
1" foam paintbrushes

1 Thoroughly wash and dry the glass shade. Paint the shade with three coats of the Copper Topper Metallic Surfacer, allowing it to dry between coats.

2 Lightly sand the wood circle. Wipe clean. Paint it with the black acrylic paint and let it dry.

3 Glue the painted glass shade onto the painted wood circle and allow it to dry overnight.

4 Drizzle the Patina Green Antiquing Solution down the sides of the glass shade. The surface will begin to change colors after about 20 minutes. Continue to drizzle with the solution until the surface is the desired color of patina green.

5 Using the black acrylic paint, lightly dab the top and around the surface randomly to give it a well-worn appearance.

C H A P T E R   8

Cleaning and Restoration

Second-hand items can be very grungy and filthy when you purchase them. A little soap and water is usually all it takes to make the item sparkling clean. However, some items may need just a little bit more help to get them into tip-top shape.

Restoring the Sparkle to Glassware

Glassware is one of my favorite things. I collect it in every shape, size, and color. I'm especially fond of Depression glass.

If your glassware has any sticky residue on it, it can be removed with rubbing alcohol, hair spray, or a commercial "goop" remover. (These products will also work on just about everything else, from wood to metal.) For the initial cleaning, line your sink with a soft towel to prevent the glassware from breaking. Fill the sink with warm, sudsy water. Let the glass items sit in this bath for about 10 minutes, and rinse them clean. Buff dry using a soft towel or a glass cloth.

Cloudy glassware can be a problem. If an item is truly old, it may never become the sparkling beauty you want it to be. This is because the glass is actually etched from years of use and abuse. Newer items that have a cloudy interior can often be cleaned and restored. Often the cloudy appearance is the result of an accumulation of lime, which is found in everyday water.

To clean a cloudy bowl, pitcher, or other vessel, fill the item 1/4 full with crushed ice (not cubes). Add the juice of one lemon and one tablespoon of salt. Swish the salt around in the vessel until the residue is gone. To clean a plate or flat item, sprinkle salt on half of a lemon and rub on the surface to clean the residue. Clean with soap and water and dry well.

Some glass items can also benefit from a soak in an ammonia solution. However, don't use ammonia on glassware that has been decorated with gold or silver. The ammonia can discolor the decoration. Line the sink with a towel, and fill

two-thirds full with warm water and add a half-cup of ammonia. Let the items sit for twenty minutes or so until clean. Wash and rinse. Dry well using a soft cloth.

I don't recommend purchasing broken glass, as gluing can be problematic. It's difficult to hide the seam. However, chipped glass rims can be repaired by rubbing with a nail file until the edge is smooth. Dab the repair with a bit of clear nail polish.

Cleaning Ceramics

There's usually not much that needs to be done to get ceramics sparkling clean. Usually it's just a case of removing some old goop on the surface. Give the item a soap and water bath and dry it well.

White stoneware can be another matter. To get old stoneware clean again, I recommend a soaking. Fill a sink with room temperature water and add one quarter cup of baking soda. Let the stoneware sit in the solution for 24 hours and check it. If it's nice and clean, rinse well and dry the items. If they're not quite clean yet, let them sit in the solution for an additional 24 to 48 hours. If they're not clean by that time, they never will be.

Sometimes a ceramic item may have a small chipped area. This can be repaired with nail polish. Choose a color to match and brush it carefully onto the spot. If the chip is only in the glazing, you can repair it with clear nail polish.

Dealing with Rust and Peeling Paint

Cleaning rust can send some folks running in panic—the same goes for peeling paint; they need not be such horrible things! Worn paint or a little rust can add charm to some items, such as old doorknobs or window frames.

Rust and peeling paint should be flaked off with a wire brush or sandpaper; clean the item thoroughly. There are several commercial rust-removers on the market that can help eliminate, or at least reduce, the appearance of rust on an item. You can also use naval jelly, but it can be messier than the stuff you're trying to remove.

A word about old paint: *Most paints made before the mid-1970s do contain lead.* The risk posed by the small items we've worked with in this book, however, is negligible. If you are concerned about lead content, you can quickly and easily seal the item against leaching by applying two to three coats of acrylic polyurethane—and be sure that curious little fingers won't have access to it.

Cleaning Metal and Plate Ware

I love old silver plate and brass. The upkeep doesn't scare me at all. I'll let you in on a little secret: You can find tons of great silver plate at thrift stores and tag sales because most folks don't want to hassle with keeping it clean. But the truth is, as long as you don't handle your silver plate all the time, the polishing will last for months. I clean my silver ware two to three times each year. I gather up all of my items, and clean and polish them one by one. I find this to be a very enjoyable task. I love the gleam of the freshly polished metal.

Use a cleaner meant for the type of metal you are polishing. You can find cleaners for silver, brass, copper, and stainless steel at any grocery store. My favorite brand of polish is Wright's. It has a creamy texture, which clings to the metal—as opposed to liquids that can drip off. It's applied using a sponge that is included with the polish.

After drying your metal items, buff them to a shine using a clean towel.

Caring for Old Textiles

Vintage textiles often have a yellow cast to them. This can usually be removed with a simple laundering and air-drying the items in the sunshine. Use a mild soap, such as Ivory® dish soap, or Woolite® Wash. If the item is white, you can also add a capful or two of liquid bleach. Don't use bleach on anything that has several colors in it, or has colorful embroidery. You don't want to fade the item!

Wash the items by hand in a sink of room-temperature water, swishing them around until clean. Rinse several times in clean water. To remove the excess water, press the item against the sides of the sink and then wrap it in a towel to remove the excess moisture. Never wring an item because it can cause damage or stretching.

If an item has an obvious grease or oil stain, you should first try to absorb as much of the oil from the fibers as possible. Sprinkle the area with a thick layer of baby powder and rub it into the fabric with your fingers. Let the powder sit on the stain overnight and launder as recommended above.

Iron the items while they are still damp. This will help you "block" them back into shape, and it's easier to remove creases when the water fattens the fibers. Never starch a vintage item until you are ready to use it. If you pre-starch the item and then fold and store it, the fabric can become damaged along the creases. Delicate linens should be wrapped in acid-free tissue before storing. Never, ever store linens directly on a wood surface, such as the inside of a cupboard—it will yellow and pick up residue from the wood finish. Instead, line the cupboard with acid-free tissue or cotton toweling.

If you encounter difficult-to-remove stains, don't despair. Iron based stains can be removed with a rust-remover product formulated for textiles. You can find them in the laundry section at the supermarket. A little goes a long way: I recommend wetting a cotton swab with the rust-removing solution and dabbing lightly over the stain.

Sometimes worn or stained areas can be camouflaged by simply covering them with another piece of linen, such as a doily. This is especially true on cushions and such—like the projects in this book.

If all else fails, why not just go with the aged, yellow look? Tea-dye the item. To tea dye, fill a bowl with hot water and several tea bags. "Dance" the teabags in the water for three to five minutes and remove the tea bags. Let the water come to room temperature. Soak the item in the tea water, checking it often until it is the desired color. Dunk the item in ice cold water to help set the stain.

Paints and Decorative Finishes

There are many different types of paints and finishes available to you. They run the gamut from rust-preventing glossy paints to those resembling stone or terra cotta. The look you want will determine the type of paint you choose.

Some items may require a primer base coat. This includes unfinished wood, most metals (unless you are using no-prep metal paints), and slick surfaces such as highly polished ceramic. Although primer dries very quickly, I do recommend waiting at least 24 hours for the primer to cure before painting.

Most of the items in this book are painted with acrylic craft paints and finishes, but some also use spray products. You can find these at craft stores and home improvement centers. I've made it a point not to include any product you would have difficulty locating.

I have also used products that can be cleaned up using ordinary soap and water. Not only are they easier to clean up, they tend to dry faster than oil-based products.

Be sure to paint (or, remove paint) in a well-ventilated area. There's nothing worse than feeling "loopy" after painting a project. I like to work outdoors—weather permitting.

Furniture Basics

If you bring home a piece of furniture that is

a little wobbly, you can easily fix the problem. Re-glue the items using wood glue (lots of it) from the home-improvement center. Hold the pieces together firmly until the glue sets, or clamp the item. Sand off any excess glue after the piece is completely dry.

For chair rungs, clamping isn't a practical solution, so I recommend you tie string around the chair legs to apply pressure to the joint. Cut the string off when the glue dries. This is my favorite way of holding things together during the gluing process. You can also use masking tape, but then you run the risk of damaging the finish when the tape is removed.

Cracks or gouges in wooden items can be repaired easily using wood putty (also known as wood dough). Smooth the putty into the gouge using a putty knife and wipe smooth with the knife. Let it dry—wood putty dries very quickly. Sand the repair with fine sandpaper after is has dried completely.

To remove shallow scratches from "junk" wood furniture that you're going to paint, place a dampened cloth over the scratch (old washrags work well). Press the cloth with a hot iron directly over the scratch. The steam will cause the scratch to lift from the surface like magic!

Adding Decorative Elements

Decorative elements can add an entirely new dimension to your finds. Scrounge around for items such as knobs and faceplates, buttons, jewels, ribbons and trims, ribbon roses, and glass beads or marbles.

Most items can be glued safely to the surface of the item using clear household cement, such as E6000. Tacky glue also works well. Whatever you use, be sure it will dry clear. Hardware should be attached using the original screws, or replace them with the exact same size of screw.

Don't glue items to fabrics; instead, stitch them in place using all-purpose thread.

Resources

NOTE: If you would like to build a similar version of the corner shelf, the pattern and instructions can be found on the Web site at **http://www.cherylfall.com**. The shelf used in this book is a vintage shelf.

Manufacturers

The following manufacturers feature specific products used in this book. I have included their Web sites where available.

DecoArt®
(Paints and finishes)
P.O. Box 386
Sanford, Kentucky 40484
800-447-8478
www.decoart.com

Delta Technical Coatings
(Paints and finishes)
2550 Pelissier Place
Whittier, California 90601
800-423-4135
www.deltacrafts.com

Walnut Hollow Farm
(Ready-to-finish woodcrafts)
1409 State Road 23
Dodgeville, Wisconsin 53533
800-950-5010
www.walnuthollow.com

Coats & Clark
(Sewing threads and trims)
Two Lake Pointe Plaza
4135 South Stream Boulevard
Charlotte, North Carolina 28217
www.coats.com

Eclectic Products, Inc.
(E6000 glue)
800-767-4667

Elmer's Products
(Glues)
PO Box 369003
Columbus, Ohio 43236-9003
www.elmers.com

American Accents
(Paints and finishes)
11 Hawthorn Parkway
Vernon Hills, Illinois 60061
800-323-3584
www.rustoleum.com

Krylon
(Paints and finishes)
800-4KRYLON
www.krylon.com

StickoPotamus
(Stickers, decals, and scrapbooking supplies)
125 Entin Road
Clifton, New Jersey 04017
973-458-0092
www.stickopotamus.com

J.A.Wright & Company
(Cream polishes for metals)
P.O. Box 566
Keene, New Hampshire 03431
800-922-2625
www.jawright.com

INDEX

Discover...Create...Decorate

Easy Heirloom Embroidery
by Cheryl Fall

Create items in the style of fine vintage linens using simple elegant stitches. Detailed stitch diagrams will guide you through all the necessary steps to create over 25 projects, many of which can be completed in a few hours. Projects include table runners, dresser scarves, a tote bag, apron, pillows, and framed art. Also included are helpful tips for collecting, cleaning and storing both old and new linens.

Softcover • 8¼x10⅞ • 144 pages
200 color photos & illus.
Item# HEMB • $24.95

Warman's® Flea Market Price Guide
3rd Edition
by Ellen T. Schroy

Great deals lie ahead when you start your flea market adventures with this updated guide. Respected antiques author, Ellen Schroy, offers invaluable preparation tips, sound collecting advice, additional reference information and completely updated pricing for today's hottest collectibles. Expanded coverage includes new categories such as Character Watches, Children's Records, Liberty Blue Dinnerware, Pet Equipment, and Lea Stein Jewelry.

Softcover • 8½x11 • 376 pages
800+ b&w photos • 8-page color section
Item# WFM3 • $21.99

Creative Containers
The Resourceful Crafter's Guide
by Jill Evans

How many times have you heard "One man's trash is another man's treasure?" Well, in this new book, author Jill Evans shows you how to turn your trash into beautiful home dÈcor items, useful containers and earth friendly gifts. From things like tuna cans, vegetable cans and cookie tins, you'll create 50 unique projects such as a scarecrow, red-nosed reindeer, penguin, candleholder and leprechaun!

Softcover • 8¼x10⅞ • 96 pages
75 color photos
Item# CRCONT • $14.95

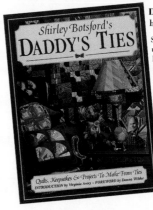

Daddy's Ties
by Shirley Botsford

Shirley Botsford unknots some creative ideas for Dad's old unused ties. Learn to make great keepsakes and one-of-a-kind gifts. Complete patterns, step-by-step instructions, a full-color illustrations show you how to make quilts, picture frames, and dozens of other beautiful treasures.

Softcover • 8¼x10⅞ • 96 pages
color throughout
Item# DADTI • $16.95

Sewing With Vintage Linens
by Samantha McNesby

Creatively construct new home dÈcor items from embroidered accessories and handkerchiefs, old quilts, vintage clothing, and more from this new reference. More than 25 projects range in complexity from simple to advanced, including handkerchief pillows, memory quilts, slipcovers, and an upholstered ottoman. Includes detailed directions and photos, a resource guide, an inspirational photo gallery, and all patterns.

Softcover • 8¼x10⅞ • 128 pages
125 color photos
Item# SWVL • $21.99

The Art of Painting Animals on Rocks
by Lin Wellford

Rock animals are fun, unique little works of art. The "canvas" is free. And with this book, anyone can paint them! Eleven step-by-step projects are included, with inspiring ideas for many more.

Softcover • 8½x11 • 128 pages
250 color illus.
Item# 30606 • $22.99

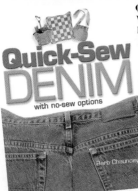

Quick-Sew Denim
With No-Sew Options
by Barb Chauncey

Transform your old denim into new, exciting projects for your home, office, or fashion accessories. This unique reference shows you how to utilize all the parts of a pair of jeans or bib overalls to create easy-to-make projects, including purses, pillows, frames, gift bags, storage containers, and desk accessories. Learn the basic techniques for gluing and sewing the different styles of denim.

Softcover • 8¼x10⅞ • 128 pages
350 color photos
Item# QSD • $21.99